Coach Guidelines —Vinton County Soccer League

Copyright © 2017 by Jannette Quackenbush

**Coach Guidelines
Vinton County Soccer League**

ISBN-10: 1-940087-22-8
ISBN-13: 978-1-940087-22-1

21 Crows Dusk to Dawn
Publishing, 21 Crows, LLC

All rights reserved. No part of this book may be reproduced or transmitted in any form or by any means, electronic or mechanical, including photocopying, recording, or by any information storage and retrieval system, without permission in writing from the copyright owner. This is a work of fiction. Names, characters, places and incidents either are the product of the author's imagination or are used fictitiously, and any resemblance to any actual persons, living or dead, events, or locales is entirely coincidental. This book was printed in the United States of America.

Vinton County Soccer League
Practice Guidelines and Information for Coaches

We are here to develop each player's skills. The emphasis is on training—and having fun.

The lessons are divided into age groups:

- **4-5 Years Old**
- **6-7 Years Old**
- **8-10 Years Old**
- **11–17 Years Old**

Each age group has four weeks of teaching tools and goals. Each week, players will be introduced to new goals and tools to learn the game of soccer along with drills for each. All information needed to teach the goals are found within the weekly teaching tools. Coaches can add their own drills and may also find that players are interested in learning more. Feel free to expand upon what is offered within these guidelines.

It is *not* imperative that they accomplish the goals to move on, only that they follow the principles and have a basic understanding of them through the games and exercises. There is no need to spend more than 2-3 minutes talking about the goals to the players. They will learn them over time and by playing the games. In other words, we want the players to learn by having fun!

THE BOOKLET COVERS:
THE BASICS OF SOCCER

The following are basic guidelines for coaches, teaching practices, weekly goals and drills.

- **Basic Warmups:**
- **Basic Rules of Soccer**
- **How to Dribble a Ball**
- **How to Kick a Ball**
- **Stopping a Ball**
- **Passing a Ball**
- **Basic Shielding**
- **Basic Fakes**
- **Soccer Positions**
- **The Job of the Goalkeeper**

Weekly Guidelines, Goals and Drills:
- **4-5 Years Old**
- **6-7 Years Old**
- **8-10 Years Old**
- **11–17 Years Old**

BASIC WARMUPS: ALWAYS WARM UP AS A TEAM BEFORE PRACTICE!

Ankles and Knees: Hands on knees. Knees bent. Rotate knees in a circular motion in one direction 5-10 times. Repeat in the opposite direction.

Hips: Stand up straight with hands on hips. Rotate hips in a circle in one direction 5-10 times. Repeat in the opposite direction five times.

Upper Body: Stand straight. Lock hands in front of the body. Bring hands forward so they touch the chest. Use arms to twist body in one direction. Repeat in the opposite direction.

Lunge: Stand straight up and extend (lunge) the right foot as far as possible. The toes of both feet are pointed forward. Bend the right knee slightly while keeping the upper body straight. The left heel stays planted on the ground. Repeat with left foot extended.

Toe Touch: Stand straight up with feet shoulder width apart. Bend forward and touch the toes. (Don't bounce.)
-Stand straight up with feet double shoulder width apart. Bend forward and touch the ground between legs.
-Stand straight up with feet double shoulder width apart and the toes of both feet pointed forward. Bend to the right. Try to touch the right foot with both hands. Straighten up. Repeat for left side.

Juggling: Juggle the ball back and forth between knees. Start with one round of knee to knee, then work up to ten. Next, juggle using your feet.

Wall Kicks: Find an outside wall that can take a bit of a beating and kick the ball at it. Start at five feet away and work up to greater lengths. Once you get the kick down, try to hit the same spot more than once.

Remember to cool down. Stretches should be done after playing as well as before. Stretching is most efficient when the muscles are warm after playing.

HOW THE GAME IS PLAYED— BASIC RULES OF SOCCER:

The Game: At the start of play, there is a kick-off. All the players must be on their defending side of the field. Only the player kicking off is allowed inside the center circle.

After the kick-off, the ball will be played until it goes out of bounds or the referee calls a penalty. The ball must *completely* cross the boundary to be out of bounds.

- You can't intentionally touch the ball with your hands or arms unless you are a goalie!
- You can't foul another player:
    - Fouling is: Tripping, pushing, un-sportsman-like behavior, touching the ball with hands or arm.
    - Penalty kicks may be awarded to the team that received the foul.
    - Offending player may receive a yellow or red card.

Kick off - At the beginning of a period, at the beginning of a game or after a goal is made. Ball is placed on the center mark and kicked by one team. (A coin toss decides the initial side of kickoff) After that, each team takes a turn.) Until the ball crosses the line, players from the attacking team may not cross the central mark and players from the defending team must be at least 10 yards from the ball. The kicker cannot kick the ball again until another player has touched the ball.

Throw in - When the whole of the ball has passed over boundary line, either by air or on the ground, it is put back into play by a throw in at the point the ball crossed the line by a player of the team opposite of the last one who touched it. The player must face the playing field with part of each foot on the touchline or on the ground outside the touchline. Part of each foot must be on the ground. Both hands must be used to throw the ball and ball must be held behind and over the head.

Coach Guidelines —Vinton County Soccer League

Corner Kick - When the ball passes completely over the defending team's goal line *and* was last touched by a *defending player* and a goal was not scored. It is put back into play by a player of the attacking team from the corner of the field nearest to where the ball crossed the boundary line.

Goal Kick- When the ball goes out of the defending team's goal line, was last touched by the *attacking team* and there was no score, it is put back into play by the defending team. They may place the ball anywhere within their Goal Box (including on the line) and then kick it.

Penalty kick: When a foul occurs in the penalty area, the fouled team is awarded a penalty kick.

Off Sides - The offensive player is offside if they are nearer to the opponent's goal line than both the second to last and last opponent and the soccer ball.

HOW TO DRIBBLE A SOCCER BALL:

One of the basic fundamentals of soccer is moving the ball from one place to another.

- Tap the ball back and forth with the insides of your shoe to push the ball forward.
- Knees should be bent
- Arms should be out for balance and to keep defenders out of the player's space
- Eyes should not be on the ball

To move the ball in a different direction:
Touch the ball with the outside of the foot with toe slightly up and ankle locked.

HOW TO KICK A SOCCER BALL:

THE BASIC KICK:

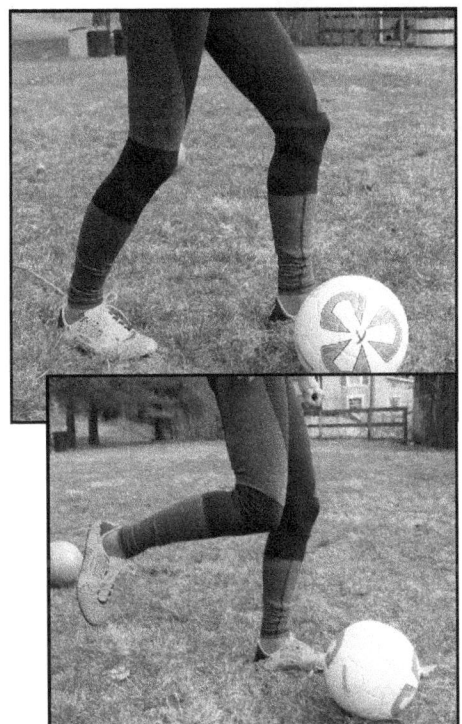

1. Look up quickly before kicking the ball
2. Look back at the ball
3. Take a large stride.
4. Have the non-shooting foot land right next to the soccer ball

5. The player whips the striking foot back.

6. **THE PLAYER STRIKES THE SOCCER BALL *WITH THE TOE POINTING DOWN AND THE BALL IS HIT WITH THE LACES*. This is important that all the players learn** this proper technique instead of just punting with the toe. (The toe kick is only used for kicks that are almost out of reach!)

A few other ways to kick the ball:

- **Instep** – To strike with power, use the top surface of the foot where the shoe laces begin.
- **Inside of the Foot** – Kick with the inside of the foot for more accuracy.
    - Or wrap the foot around the ball, cupping it.
- **Outside of the Foot** - Use the outer surface of the front part of your foot to strike the center of the ball.
- **The Volley** – a strike as the ball is coming to you and out of the air.
- **The Toe - only** if you have to stretch for the ball, use the toe to kick it.

Tricks to help players focus on the basic kick:

1. Have the players sit on the ground and take off the kicking foot cleat and sock.
    - Place both feet on the ground.
    - Place arms around knees.
    - Hold the ball between the knees with the hands and gently kick the ball lightly a couple feet above the knees at the laces. It should go up straight and not spin. If it spins, the ball is being kicked on one side or the other and not straight.
    - Toes should be pointed.
    - Ankle should be locked

2. Have the players stand next and kick the ball up into the air about three feet over their heads until they get the control of the ball.

3. Now, have them kick back and forth with another player.

Coach Guidelines —Vinton County Soccer League

STOPPING THE BALL:

Players can stop a ball with: the inside or outside of the foot, heel, shin, thigh, stomach, chest, shoulder or head.

Upper Body: When the ball impacts with the upper body from the air, simply relax the part of your body which is going to stop the ball and move slightly backwards to absorb the impact.

The Feet: When the ball is ready to have contact with the foot, lean slightly on the opposite leg.

As the ball reaches the cleat, move the foot gently back to absorb the impact. Player can stop the ball with the inside of the foot, the outside of the foot or by absorbing the impact with the toe on top of the ball.

PASSING THE BALL:

Players work together, kicking the ball short and long distances to an opponent's goal.

1. **Standard Pass**: For shorter distances. Player turns the hip outward and lifts leg to the side. The ball is passed with the inside of the foot. Body should be pointed toward the teammate. This is the pass used most often when the ball is on the ground.
2. **Lofted Pass**: For long distances. Place the left foot. Kick the bottom of the ball with the right at the knuckle of the big toe (lacing area)
3. **Push Pass**: Player uses the instep of the cleat (at the arch) and along the arch to push the ball in a forward motion.

BASIC SHIELDING

It is important to learn good shielding techniques to keep the opponent from stealing the ball, and to protect the space around the player.

Shields are used when it is simply too difficult to continue dribbling the ball past an opponent (there are either too many opponents near or the opponent blocks the course).

The basic shielding posture is:

- Knees should be bent
- Arms bent and out to sides

The 4 Steps to Shielding:

Shielding the ball keeps the opposing team players from stealing the ball. The four basic shielding moves are:

1. **Simple step across** - The player steps over the ball to put either one or both legs between the ball and an opponent. Player is trying to place themselves in the best position to pass to another teammate.

2. **The roll -** Player moves the ball around either with the side of the foot or the bottom of the foot.

3. **The pull-back–** With the pullback move, the ball is pulled or rolled to one side using the bottom of the foot. Start with the ball between your feet. Make a fake motion of kicking the ball with the right foot. Then instead of kicking, stop the ball with the bottom of your shoe to the top of the ball. Then pull back the ball by scraping the cleats backwards to get the ball rolling to the right and behind.

4. **The circle turn** - There are two basic types of circle turns - the first is using the inside of the foot and a second, using the outside of the foot. The ball is tapped with the foot in the opposite direction of the opponent and in a circular motion.

FAKES:

Fake Kick Inside (Pretend to kick, instead kick to inside)

Fake Kick Outside (Pretend to kick, instead kick to outside)

While ball is being dribbled, the left foot is planted near the ball. The right is wound up as if to kick. Instead of kicking the ball, the right leg is brought down in a chopping motion to cut the ball to either direction. If it is moved with the outside of the foot, it is a fake kick outside. If it is moved with the inside, it is a fake kick inside.

Pull backs.

- **Turn with Pullback**
- **Turn Away with Pullback**

Start with the ball between your feet. Make a fake motion of kicking the ball with the right foot. Then instead of kicking, stop the ball with the bottom of your shoe to the top of the ball. Pull back the ball by scraping the cleats backwards to get the ball rolling to the right and behind. If you used your right foot to "pull-back" and you turn *clockwise* or towards the pull-back leg it is a "turn-with pull-back". If your turn is *counterclockwise* away from the right leg, it is a "turn-away pull-back".

The Step over.

When dribbling the ball toward the opponent, player steps *over* the ball with the right foot and appears to be heading left. (Foot will land to the left of the ball) As the opponent goes to the left, the outside of the right foot is equal to the ball and is used to push the ball to the right.

Step over 180

Player starts with ball between feet. With weight on left leg, the right foot is swung over the ball while turning counter clockwise to the left. Then, the right foot is placed down on the left side of the ball. Ultimately, the right foot is used to pivot, spin around with the left foot back toward the ball. After turning 180, take the ball with the left foot and move in either direction.

MORE DRIBBLING TOOLS AND FAKES:

While dribbling, a player will need to maneuver around an opponent. When things get tight, they can use fakes to *out*maneuver the opponent—

The Swerve: Player approaches opponent on left, then makes a quick dodge to the right using the outside of the right foot to tap the ball in that direction.

The Stop and Go.

While dribbling next to an opponent, the ball is stopped with a tap on top with the sole of the right foot. The body however, appears to be going toward the left even though the right foot appears to be heading right. As opponent steps to the left, the right foot is dropped and the player taps the ball with the right foot and bursts past.

The Fake Shot.

Pull the leg back as if you are readying to kick the ball in one direction, then stop motion before kicking it in the opposite direction.

The Cut Back.

While dribbling to the left of an opponent, player uses the inside of the foot to cut the ball back behind the body. Player plants the left foot to the side of the ball and then brings the right foot up to cut the ball back.

Inside Cut

While dribbling the ball toward an opponent, player reaches the foot around the front of the ball and cuts it backwards with the inside of your foot.

Inside Outside.

Player fakes going inside, then rushes to the outside. The inside of the player's foot is used to carry the ball to the inside, then when the opponent is off-balance, player can shoot or continue dribbling.

Outside Cut

Player uses the outside of the foot to cut the ball back in the other direction. Standing foot is planted far enough away from the ball so player can pivot away, turning hips and body and cut the ball with the outside of the foot in one motion.

Dropping The Shoulder.

Player dribbles slowly to the opponent, dipping the shoulder down and taking off in the opposite direction.

Sole of the foot turn.

Player pulls the ball back with the bottom of the shoe then bursts away.

Scoop.

Player scoops the ball over the opponent's foot, then rushes in the direction of the scoop.

Lunge

Player swings the foot just in front of the ball to the outside. Then player fakes going to the left by lunging with the left foot to the left. Ball is then taken away with the outside of the right foot to the right.

SOCCER POSITIONS EXPLAINED:

Each player position has a specific task, from defending against opponent attacks to scoring.

Forwards are positioned nearest to the opposing team's goal. They are the attackers used to move the ball forward and score goals. Forwards need to be fast dribblers and be agile.

Midfielders play the middle field. Their position is both offensive and defensive. They must be able to dribble the ball and also pass to the forwards and also stop an opponent's attack.

Defenders are the closest to their own goal. Their job is to stop the other team from scoring a goal. Strong kicks are a must for defenders to get the ball out of the scoring area.

Goalkeepers protect the goal and the last line of defense against the opposing team scoring.

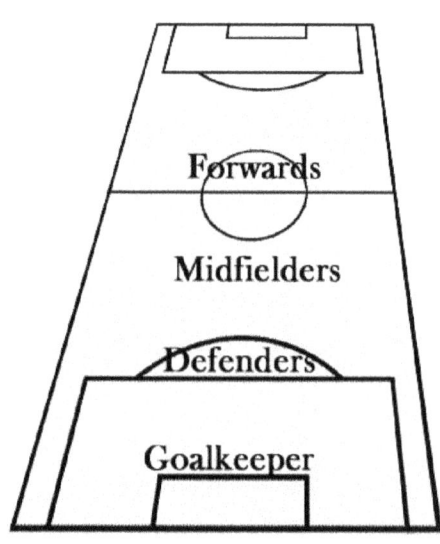

THE JOB OF THE GOALKEEPER:

The Goalkeeper's main job is to stop the ball from getting through the net. Focus is a key strategy, not only when the ball is close, but also when it is on the other end of the field. A keeper can only handle the ball inside his/her own penalty area (the rectangular area in front of and within the goal post).

How a Goalkeeper Catches/Stops a Ball in the air:

1. Keep hands moving together. Both should be behind the ball with thumbs close together.

2. Elbows should be in front of the chest.

3. Get behind the ball. When reaching for a ball, the arms should be extended out (elbows not locked!), the elbows bent as the catch is made, allowing the arms to absorb the speed and energy of the ball. Hands should be in the "W" hand position.

4. **The Standing Goalkeeper Stance**- The Goalkeeper should be always bouncing on the balls of the feet. On the ground, Goalkeeper should lower one knee close without touching the ground while picking up ball.

5. The ball may need to be hugged to the chest to protect it.

If the ball is on the ground:

The basket catch is used for balls below the waist or on the ground.

The hands are behind the ball, but the pinky fingers are together so the ball is cupped when it rolls in.

Fingers may need to brush the ground to catch the ball.

The ball can be caught with the legs straight.

Or knees bent.

Or kneeling.

Goalkeeper Drills:
- Practice toss a ball, some high and some low, catching the ball by throwing it back and forth between players.
- Discuss that it is a team effort to protect the ball and not the Goalkeeper's fault if he/she misses and the other team gets a point.
- Sideways shuffling between cones or quick steps forward and backwards between cones to practice covering the goal area.
- Have one player be the goalkeeper. Divide players up into two sides and set up six cones on either side so each group can race to traverse the cones and try to take a shot into the goal.
- One player kicks the ball toward the other player who makes a sideways dive to catch the ball.
- One player rolls the ball toward the other who stops and picks up the ball.
- Goalkeeper takes a turn kicking ball out of their hands and for the other player to catch.

WEEKLY GUIDELINES FOR COACHING

4-5 Years Old
6-7 Years Old
8-10 Years Old
11–17 Years Old

COACHING 4-5 YEAR OLDS

COACHING 4-5 YEAR OLDS

This age group is just learning to socialize and share. It is important to take a lot of breaks and give brief directions. Top priority is getting used to the ball.

The main objective of coaching the youngest league is to teach the very basics—kicking the ball with their feet and not picking the ball up with their hands. One of the hardest parts of coaching the players is trying to keep them from bunching up to get the ball or trying to keep one player from taking the ball while a pack follows far behind. Simply put, it may not happen!

Coaches will be allowed to walk along the inside of the sidelines on the field and within the field with the players during the games to guide them, if needed. Please don't hesitate to encourage the players verbally—reminding them to use their feet to kick the ball and showing them which way to run toward the goal.

Players who kick or hit another player will be given a "time out" for three minutes. Please take a moment to gently explain the violation. If the issues continue, we do have support and resources to help our coaches work with players with special needs. Please remember above all to have fun with the players and don't be afraid to jump right in with them to have that fun!

Ball Size: 3
Recommended Field Sizes: 25 X 30 or 50 X 30
Goal Size: 6 feet high X 18 wide or 4 feet X 4 feet
Match Duration—4 (6-8 minutes)

These are just basic guidelines. Feel free to use your own tools to help the players understand by games and drills! The basic goals you are attempting to achieve with this age group are:

- Learning to kick the ball without using hands
- Learning to run toward the correct goal post with verbal guidance
- Learning to listen to the coach and/or referee
- Learning to work with opponents and teammates without pushing or kicking. (Good sportsmanship!)
- Learning to stay with teammates and coach when waiting on the bench to play instead of staying with family—**players must stay with the coach!**
- Learning to pass to a teammate with verbal guidance

Field Layout: 3 X 3

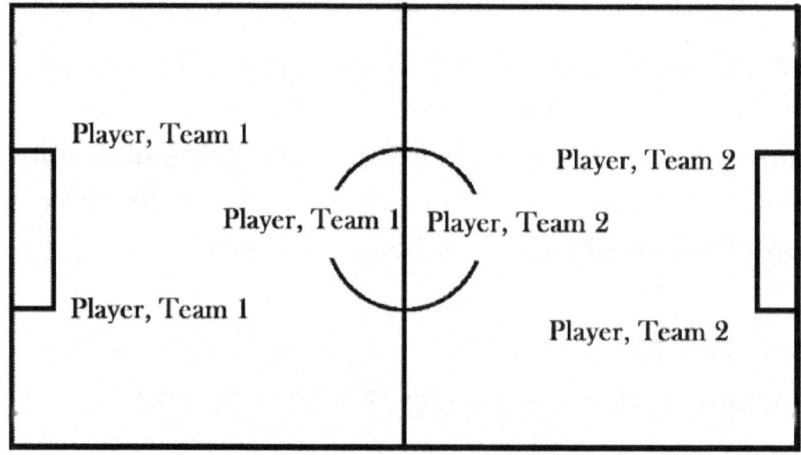

THE LESSONS:

The lessons are divided into four weeks. Each week, players will be introduced to a new goal. It is *not* imperative that they accomplish the goals to move on, only that they follow the principles and have a basic understanding of them through the games and exercises. There is no need to spend more than 2-3 minutes talking about the goals to the players. TEACH BY PLAYING GAMES. They will learn the techniques over time and by playing the games. In other words, we want the players to learn by having fun!

Remember that players learn goals at different stages. Some learn a certain goal early and others may take more time. Every player may not be able to accomplish all the goals by the end of the season. Our main purpose is to offer the goal and let them learn by having fun.

Week 1—Ages 4-5

Goals:
1. Warm up
2. Learn how to dribble the ball
3. Learn how to kick the ball

Teaching Tool:

HOW TO DRIBBLE A SOCCER BALL:

One of the basic fundamentals of soccer is moving the ball from one place to another.

- Tap the ball back and forth with the insides of your shoe to push the ball forward.
- Knees should be bent
- Arms should be out for balance and to keep defenders out of the player's space
- Eyes should not be on the ball

To move the ball in a different direction:

Touch the ball with the outside of the foot with toe slightly up and ankle locked.

Drill:

- Set up cones and have the players run between them dribbling the ball.
- Walk the Dog—Scatter cones or cups around the field. Have each player take a ball and give it a dog name. Then, tell them the cones (or cups) are trees and they have to walk to each tree to let the dog

(ball) sniff. However, if you yell BIG DOG, they have to run while dribbling their balls to the safety of the goal posts.
- Play Duck Duck Goose with a soccer ball
- Hit the Coach—set up four cones and have the players dribble the ball between the cones and try to kick the ball at your legs. If they hit you, they call out an animal and you have to make the animal sound.
- Red Light, Green light—Coach stands in the center of the field. The players, each with a ball, stand at the Goal post. Coach calls out green light and the players dribble until yellow light (they have to slow) or red light (they have to stop) is called.
- Sharks and Minnows-Make half the players minnows and half the players sharks. Put the minnows at one end of a field and sharks in the center. Give each of the minnows a ball and tell them they have to get past the sharks to the other end of the field without the sharks taking their ball and kicking it off the field. If a minnow loses the ball, he/she becomes a shark and must try to steal the balls.

Teaching Tool:

LEARN TO KICK THE BALL

Show the players how to kick the ball with their feet. Have them hold their hands crossed over their chest, if needed, to remind them not to use their hands.

HOW TO KICK A SOCCER BALL:

THE BASIC KICK:

1. Look up quickly before kicking the ball
2. Look back at the ball
3. Take a large stride.
4. Have the non-shooting foot land right next to the soccer ball
5. The player whips the striking foot back.

6. **THE PLAYER STRIKES THE SOCCER BALL *WITH THE TOE POINTING DOWN AND THE BALL IS HIT WITH THE LACES*. This is important that all the players learn this proper technique instead of just punting with the toe. (The toe kick is only used for kicks that are almost out of reach!) You may have to physically hold the foot of each child in front of the ball to show them the correct position.**

Drills:

- Play kick the cone. Place cones in front of the goal box. Have the players take 4-5 steps back and take turns kicking the ball toward the goal posts to see if they can knock over a cone.
- Place the players in two lines facing each other. Give them one ball to kick back and forth to the players in the line in front of them.
- Between the cones: Set out two cones and have the players stand back about five feet. The object is to gently kick the ball through the cones. Have them use the inside of their foot to do this.
- Feel free to add more games of your own!

Week 2 —Ages 4-5

Goals:
1. Go over warm-ups
2. Learn to kick toward/into the goal
3. Learn where to line up during the game. (basic positioning)

Teaching Tool:
Show the players where the goals are. Tell them the object of the game is to get the ball through the goal posts. The players will not understand positions. Instead show them where they stand in 2-3 lines behind the center line. Show them which direction they will run on the field and tell them you will be there to point them toward the correct goal and in the right direction during the games.

Drill:
- Have the players race from one goal post to the other.
- Place a ball in front of the goal, have the players practice kicking the ball between the posts.
- Place several balls four steps in front of the goal posts. Take the players to the opposite end of the field and let them race down to kick the balls between the posts.
- Place several balls four steps in front of the goal posts. Take the players to the middle of the field and let them race down to kick the balls between the

posts.

- Give each of the players a ball. Have them dribble on one side of the field, staying inbounds and trying to kick the ball away from others.
- Red Light, Green light—Coach stands at the goal post. The players, each with a ball, stand at the opposite goal post. Coach calls out green light and the players dribble until yellow light (they have to slow) or red light (they have to stop) is called. They try to get their ball past the goal posts and the coach.

WEEK 3—AGES 4-5

Goals:
1. Go over warm-ups
2. Learn how to pass the ball

Teaching Tool:

PASSING THE BALL:
Basic Passing:

- Make sure the players understand they cannot hit, shove or kick another player even if they are mad at them.
- Show the players how to properly gently kick the ball with their foot to another player

Players work together, kicking the ball short and long distances to an opponent's goal.

1. **Standard Pass**: For shorter distances. Player turns the hip outward and lifts leg to the side. The ball is passed with the inside of the foot. Body should be pointed toward the teammate. This is the pass used most often when the ball is on the ground.

Drill:
- Have the players race from one goal post to the other.
- Give each player a ball and have them gently tap the ball with the inside of their feet for five or six steps.

Also do this from one goal post to the other.
- Place the players in random formations and have them dribble without touching other players. When you call out a body part (inside of foot, outside of foot, heel, toes.) the players must stop the ball with that body part.
- Make a circle and let the players kick the ball to each other in the circle.
- Red Light, Green light—Coach stands at the goal Post. The players, each with a ball, stand at the opposite goal post. Coach calls out green light and the players dribble until yellow light (they have to slow) or red light (they have to stop) is called. They try to get their ball past the goal posts and the coach.
- Feel free to add more games of your own!

Week 4—Ages 4-5

Goals:

1. Go over warm-ups.
2. Learn basic sportsmanship and the importance of being in a team.
3. What it is like to play a game—scrimmage

Drill:

- Divide the players into two groups. Have each group hold hands so they are forming a wall. Toss a ball down the middle and have the players try to keep the ball moving without letting go of hands. They must all work together to keep the ball moving.
- Play Duck Duck Goose with a soccer ball
- Hit the Coach—set up four cones and have the players dribble the ball between the cones and try to kick the ball at your legs. If they hit you, they call out an animal and you have to make the animal sound.
- Red Light, Green light—Coach stands in the center of the field. The players, each with a ball, stand at the Goal post. Coach calls out green light and the players dribble until yellow light (they have to slow) or red light (they have to stop) is called.
- Sharks and Minnows-Make half the players minnows and half the players sharks. Put the minnows at one end of a field and sharks in the center. Give each of the minnows a ball and tell them they have to get past the sharks to the other end of the field without the sharks taking their ball and kicking it off the field. If a minnow loses the ball, he/she becomes a shark and must try to steal the balls.

COACHING
6-7 YEAR OLDS

COACHING 6-7 YEAR OLDS

The main objectives of coaching players 6-7 years of age is reinstating proper kicking and dribbling of the ball and developing both basic techniques of keeping the ball in possession and learning to work together as a team. At this age, they will begin understanding which direction their own goal is and begin stopping the ball with their legs. They will also be guided in understanding goal kick, corner kick, kick off and throw in and when the ball is "in" or "out" of play. Although not emphasized too greatly, players in this age group should begin to learn the different positions on the field.

Ball Size: 3 or 4
Recommended Field Sizes: 35 X 40 or 80 X 60
Goal Size: 6 feet high X 18 wide or 12 feet X 24 feet
Match Duration—4 (8 minutes)

The basic goals you are attempting to achieve with this age group are:

- Reinstating the proper way to shoot and dribble the ball
- Understanding possession of the ball and how to stop an oncoming ball.
- Developing basic techniques to keep possession of the ball while dribbling.
- Learning to work together as a team in passing and defending.
- Team support when defending and attacking and giving each other space to play.

Field Layout:

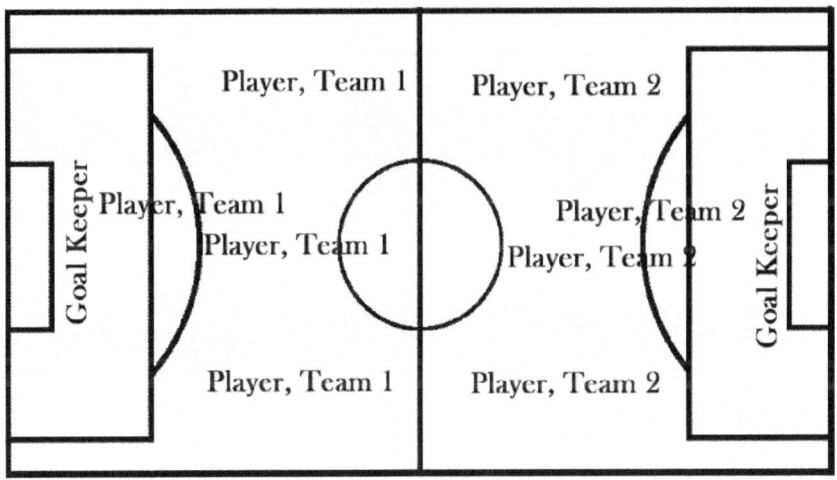

THE LESSONS:

The lessons are divided into four weeks. Each week, players will be introduced to a new goal. It is *not* imperative that they accomplish the goals to move on, only that they follow the principles and have a basic understanding of them through the games and exercises. There is no need to spend more than 2-3 minutes talking about the goals to the players. They will learn them over time and by playing the games. In other words, we want the players to learn by having fun!

Remember that players learn goals at different stages. Some learn a certain goal early and others may take more time. Every player may not be able to accomplish all the goals by the end of the season. Our main purpose is to offer the goal and let them learn by having fun.

Week 1—Ages 6-7

Goals:
1. Warm ups
2. Go over the proper way to dribble, kick, and pass the ball.
3. Learning to be the one to take control of the ball.
4. Don't hold back when you run toward the ball even if an opponent is almost to the ball.

Teaching Tool:

HOW TO DRIBBLE A SOCCER BALL:
One of the basic fundamentals of soccer is moving the ball from one place to another.

- Tap the ball back and forth with the insides of your shoe to push the ball forward.
- Knees should be bent
- Arms should be out for balance and to keep defenders out of the player's space
- Eyes should not be on the ball

To move the ball in a different direction:
Touch the ball with the outside of the foot with toe slightly up and ankle locked.

Drill:
- Have the players dribble between cones toward the goal and try to shoot a goal. Place the players in random formations and have them dribble without touching other players. When you call out a body

part (inside of foot, outside of foot, heel, toes.) the players must stop the ball with that body part.
- Make a circle and let the players kick the ball to each other in the circle.
- Red Light, Green light—Coach stands at the goal Post. The players, each with a ball, stand at the opposite goal post. Coach calls out green light and the players dribble until yellow light (they have to slow) or red light (they have to stop) is called. They try to get their ball past the goal posts and the coach.

Teaching Tool:

HOW TO KICK A SOCCER BALL:

THE BASIC KICK:

1. Look up quickly before kicking the ball
2. Look back at the ball
3. Take a large stride.
4. Have the non-shooting foot land right next to the soccer ball
5. The player whips the striking foot back.
6. **THE PLAYER STRIKES THE SOCCER BALL *WITH THE TOE POINTING DOWN AND THE BALL IS HIT WITH THE LACES*. This is important that all the players learn this proper technique instead of just punting with the toe. (The toe kick is only used for kicks that are almost out of reach!) You may have to physically hold the foot of each child in front of the ball to show them the correct position.**

The proper set up for a kick:

Drill:

- Play kick the cone. Place cones in front of the goal box. Have the players take 4-5 steps back and take turns kicking the ball toward the goal posts to see if they can knock over a cone.
- Place the players in two lines facing each other. Give them one ball to kick back and forth to the players in the line in front of them. Stand halfway across the field with your foot on the ball, barely holding it. Have each player, one by one, come up and kick the ball from your foot. Do not try to stop them. After they have done this a couple times, start at the center of the field, dribble the ball toward them and have each player run toward you and take it away. Next, pair them up and let them practice attacking and taking the ball.

Teaching Tool:

PASSING THE BALL:
Players work together, kicking the ball short and long distances to an opponent's goal.

1. **Standard Pass**: For shorter distances. Player turns the hip outward and lifts leg to the side. The ball is passed with the inside of the foot. Body should be pointed toward the teammate. This is the pass used most often when the ball is on the ground.

Drill:
- Have the players stand in a circle and kick the ball to each other. When the ball comes to them, they call out their name.

Week 2—Ages 6-7

Goals:
1. Learn how to stop the ball.
2. Stopping the ball when it is coming to the player using the foot. Then dribbling the ball after it is stopped.
3. Learn how to turn and dribble the ball to keep away from an opponent.

Teaching Tool:

Show the players how to use their bodies to stop the balls (No hands or heads!)

STOPPING A BALL:

Players can stop a ball with: the inside or outside of the foot, heel, shin, thigh, stomach, chest, shoulder or head.

Upper Body: When the ball impacts with the upper body from the air, relax the part of your body which is going to stop the ball and move slightly backwards to absorb the impact.

The Feet: When the ball is ready to impact with the foot, lean slightly on the opposite leg. AS the ball reaches the cleat, move the foot gently back to absorb the impact. Player can stop the ball with the inside of the foot, the outside of the foot or by absorbing the impact with the toe on top of the ball.

Drill:

- Show the players how to stop the ball. Give each player a ball and have them practice stopping. Next, gently kick the ball to them and have each take a turn stopping the ball. The players can also be paired and practice passing the ball and stopping it with their feet. You can also set up cones and have them dribble after each stop.
- Give each of the players a ball and have them dribble around cones. You can also take the place of a cone and reach out as if to tag the player as he or she passes

Week 3—Ages 6-7

Goals:
- Learn how to shield the ball
- Learn how and where the different positions are set up during a game. (Attackers, midfields and Defenders) (Remember, teach the roles of each player to all players! All players should play each position)
- Learning to work together as a team in passing and defending.

Teaching Tool:

BASIC SHIELDING

It is important to learn good shielding techniques to keep the opponent from stealing the ball, and to protect the space around the player.

Shields are used when it is simply too difficult to continue dribbling the ball past an opponent (there are either too many opponents near or the opponent blocks the path.)

The basic shielding posture is:

- Knees should be bent
- Arms bent and out to sides

The 4 Steps to Shielding:

Shielding the ball keeps the opponent from stealing the ball. The four basic shielding moves are:

1. **Simple step across** - The player steps over the ball to put either one or both legs between the ball and an incoming opponent. Player is trying to place themselves in the best position to pass to teammates.

2. **The roll -** Player moves the ball around either with the side of the foot or the sole of the foot.

3. **The pull-back–** With the pullback move, the ball is pulled or rolled to one side using the bottom of the foot. Start with the ball between your feet. Make a fake motion of kicking the ball with the right foot. Then instead of kicking, stop the ball with the bottom of your shoe to the top of the ball. Then pull back the ball by scraping the cleats backwards to get the ball rolling to the right and behind.

4. **The circle turn** - There are two types of circle turns - one by using the inside of the foot and one by using the outside of the foot. The ball is tapped with the foot in the opposite direction of the opponent and in a circle.

Teaching Tool:

SOCCER POSITIONS EXPLAINED:

Each player position has a specific task, from defending against opponent attacks to scoring.

Forwards are positioned nearest to the opposing team's goal. They are the attackers used to move the ball forward and score goals. Forwards need to be fast dribblers and be agile.

Midfielders play the middle field. Their position is both offensive and defensive. They must be able to dribble the ball and pass to the forwards and also stop an opponent's attack.

Defenders are the closest to their own goal. Their job is to stop the other team from scoring a goal. Strong kicks are a must for defenders to get the ball out of the scoring area.

Goalkeepers protect the goal and the last line of defense against the opposing team scoring.

Drill:

- Place cones on the field at each different position. Walk to the cones and explain each of the different positions. Players will be able to try all the positions at this age and should be shifted from position to position.
- Play Soccer Tag-Have one player dribble the ball and try to tag the others with the ball. Whoever gets tagged, is "it".
- Play a scrimmage game. Every 2-3 minutes, have players change positions with your calling out the names of the positions each will take. Make sure all the players get a short chance at playing goalkeeper.

Week 4—Ages 6-7

Goals:
1. Developing basic techniques to keep possession of the ball while dribbling.
2. Developing a basic understanding kick off, goal kick, corner kick, kick off and throw in and when the ball is in or out of play.

Teaching Tool:
- Go over Basic Shielding. Show players how to shield the ball with the body.
- Show the players each of the different kicks/throw in when the ball is out of play.

Kick off - At the beginning of a period, at the beginning of a game or after a goal is made. Ball is placed on the center mark and kicked by one team. Until the ball crosses the line, players from the attacking team may not cross the central mark and players from the defending team must be at least 10 yards from the ball. The kicker cannot kick the ball again until another player has touched the ball.

Throw in - When the whole of the ball has passed over a touch line, either by air or on the ground, it is put back into play by a throw in at the point the ball crossed the line by a player of the team opposite of the last one who touched it. The player must face the playing field with part of each foot on the touchline or on the ground outside the touchline. Part of each foot must be on the ground. Both hands must be used to throw the ball and ball must be held behind and over the head.

Corner Kick - When the ball passes completely over the defending team's goal line and was last touched by a *defending player* and a goal was not scored. It is put back into play by a player of the attacking team from the corner of the field nearest to where the ball crossed.

Goal Kick- When the ball goes out of the defending team's goal line, was last touched by the *attacking team* and there was no score, it is put back into play by the defending team. They may place the ball anywhere within their Goal Box (including on the line) and then kick it.

Penalty kick: When a foul occurs in the penalty area, the fouled team is awarded a penalty kick.

Off Sides - The offensive player is offside if they are nearer to the opponent's goal line than both the second to last and last opponent and the soccer ball.

Drill:
- Play Soccer Tag-Have one player dribble the ball and try to tag the others with the ball. Whoever gets tagged, is "it".
- Play a scrimmage game. Every 2-3 minutes, have players change positions with your calling out the names of the positions each will take. Make sure all the players get a short chance at playing goalkeeper.

COACHING
8-10 YEAR OLDS

Coaching 8-10 Year Olds

The main objectives of coaching players 8-10 years of age is giving them a more guided understanding of the rules of the game, reinstating proper kicking and dribbling of the ball and developing basic techniques of keeping the ball in possession, intro to faking and learning to work together as a team.

At this age, they will learn the basic concepts of goalkeeping and protecting the goal. They will also be guided in understanding goal kick, corner kick, kick off and throw in and when the ball is "in" or "out" of play. They will learn about different positions on the field and gain an understanding of each of these positions.

Ball Size: 4
Recommended Field Sizes: 35 X 40 or 80 X 60
Goal Size: 6 feet high X 18 wide or 12 feet X 24 feet
Match Duration—4 (6-8 minutes)

The basic goals you are attempting to achieve with this age group are:

1. Reinstating the proper way to shoot and dribble the ball
2. Understanding possession of the ball and how to stop an oncoming ball.
3. Developing basic techniques to keep possession of the ball while dribbling.
4. Developing an understanding of Goalkeeper skills.
5. Learning to work together as a team in passing

and defending.
6. Learning the basics of shielding the ball.
7. Learning positions to be played and learning to play those positions.
8. Team support when defending and attacking and giving each other space to play.

Field 7 X 7

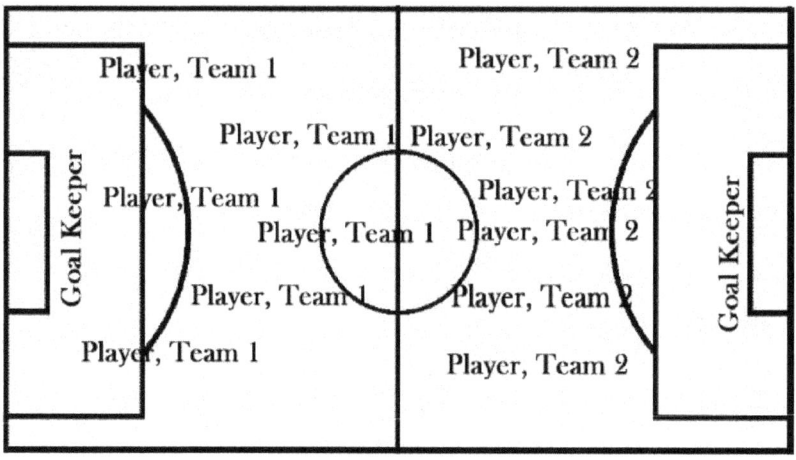

Field 5 X 5

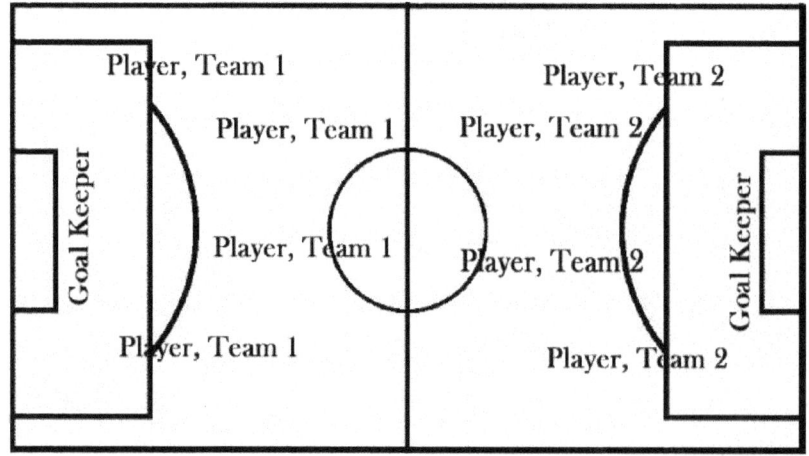

THE LESSONS:

The lessons are divided into four weeks. Each week, players will be introduced to a new goal. It is *not* imperative that they accomplish the goals to move on, only that they follow the principles and have a basic understanding of them through the games and exercises. There is no need to spend more than 2-3 minutes talking about the goals to the players. They will learn them over time and by playing the games. In other words, we want the players to learn by having fun!

Remember that players learn goals at different stages. Some learn a certain goal early and others may take more time. Every player may not be able to accomplish all the goals by the end of the season. Our main purpose is to offer the goal and let them learn by having fun.

Week 1—Ages 8-10

Goals:
1. Warm up
2. Go over the proper way to kick and pass.
3. Learn how to stop the ball—Stopping the ball when it is coming to the player using the foot. Then dribbling the ball after it is stopped.
4. Understanding possession of the ball—Don't hold back when you run toward the ball even if an opponent is almost to the ball
5. Learn first steps in Shielding :

Teaching Tool:

HOW TO KICK A SOCCER BALL:
THE BASIC KICK:

1. Look up quickly before kicking the ball
2. Look back at the ball
3. Take a large stride and plant the foot you are not going to use to kick the ball.
4. Swing your arms

5. Bring your kicking leg back, lock your ankle and kick. Use the top surface area of your shoe (big toe knuckle) just before the area the laces begin.

A few other ways to kick the ball:

- **Instep** – To strike with power, use the top surface of the foot where the shoe laces begin.
- **Inside of the Foot** – Kick with the inside of the foot for more defined accuracy.
    - Or wrap the foot around the ball, cupping it.
- **Outside of the Foot** - Use the outer surface of the front part of your foot to strike the center of the ball.
- **The Volley** – a Strike when the ball is coming to you and out of the air.
- **The Toe** If you have to stretch for the ball, use the toe to kick it.

Drill:
- Line up players across from each other and have them kick the ball back and forth to each other
- Line up cones in front of the goal and have players dribble through the cones and shoot from different distances.

Teaching Tool:

Passing the Ball:
Players work together, kicking the ball short and long distances to an opponent's goal.

1. **Standard Pass**: For shorter distances. Player turns the hip outward and lifts leg to the side. The ball is

passed with the inside of the foot. Body should be pointed toward the teammate. This is the pass used most often when the ball is on the ground.
2. **Lofted Pass**: For longer distances. Place the left foot. Kick the bottom of the ball with the right at the knuckle of the big toe.
3. **Push Pass**: Player uses the instep of the cleat (at the arch) and along the arch to push the ball in a forward motion.

Drill: Line players up and have them pass the ball back and forth. Cones can be lined up on both sides so they have to dribble certain distances before a pass.

Teaching Tool:

HOW TO STOP A BALL:

Players can stop a ball with: the inside or outside of the foot, heel, shin, thigh, stomach, chest, shoulder or head.

Upper Body: When the ball impacts with the upper body from the air, relax the part of your body which is going to stop the ball and move slightly backwards to absorb the impact.

The Feet: When the ball is ready to impact with the foot, lean slightly on the opposite leg. AS the ball reaches the cleat, move the foot gently back to absorb the impact. Player can stop the ball with the inside of the foot, the outside of the foot or by absorbing the impact with the toe on top of the ball.

Drill: Set players up in two lines and have them kick the ball back and forth and also tossing the ball to each other, practicing the stopping techniques.

Teaching Tool:

First Steps of Shielding:

BASIC SHIELDING

It is important to learn good shielding techniques to keep the opponent from stealing the ball, and to protect the space around the player.

Shields are used when it is simply too difficult to continue dribbling the ball past an opponent (there are either too many opponents near or the opponent blocks the course).

The basic shielding posture is:
- Knees should be bent
- Arms bent and out to sides

There are four types of shielding. The first to learn is:

1. **Simple step across** - The player steps over the ball to put either one or both legs between the ball and an incoming opponent. Player is trying to place themselves in the best position to pass to teammates.

Drill:
- Each player dribbles the ball along a set of cones and meets another player at the far end who tries to steal the ball. The first player uses the simple step across to block the opponent.

- Have the players race from one goal post to the other.
- Play kick the cone. Place cones in front of the goal box. Have the players take 4-5 steps back and take turns kicking the ball toward the goal posts to see if they can knock over a cone.
- Place the players in two lines facing each other. Give them one ball to kick back and forth to the players in the line in front of them.
- Stand halfway across the field with your foot on the ball, barely holding it. Have each player, one by one, come up and kick the ball from your foot. Do not try to stop them. After they have done this a couple times, start at the center of the field, dribble the ball toward them and have each player run toward you and take it away. Next, pair them up and let them practice attacking and taking the ball.

Week 2—Ages 8-10

Goals:

1. Learn how to shield the ball in order to keep a nearby opponent from stealing it. Learn Second Shield Steps
2. Learn how and where the different positions are set up during a game. (Remember, teach the roles of each position to all players!)
3. Understand the role of goalkeeper - using hands and body to defend goal.

BASIC SHIELDING

Go over the simple step across from practice 1:

1. **Simple step across** - The player steps over the ball to put either one or both legs between the ball and an incoming opponent. Player is trying to place themselves in the best position to pass to teammates.

The second shielding practice is:

2. **The roll -** Player moves the ball around either with the side of the foot or the sole of the foot.

Drill:

- Give each of the players a ball and have them slowly step over the ball while it is in place. Once they step over, have them put their backs to you as if you are the opponent. Next, have each practice stepping over the ball and turning with their back to you as you roll it toward them. After that, have them do the same drill but then they dribble it away. They can then practice with another teammate.

Teaching Tool:

Soccer Positions Explained:

Each player position has a specific task, from defending against opponent attacks to scoring.

Forwards are positioned nearest to the opposing team's goal. They are the attackers used to move the ball forward and score goals. Forwards need to be fast dribblers and be agile.

Midfielders play the middle field. Their position is both offensive and defensive. They must be able to dribble the ball and pass to the forwards and also stop an opponent's attack.

Defenders are the closest to their own goal. Their job is to stop the other team from scoring a goal. Strong kicks are a must for defenders to get the ball out of the scoring area.

Goalkeepers protect the goal and the last line of defense against the opposing team scoring.

Drill: Place cones on the field at each different position. Walk to the cones and explain each of the different positions. Players will be able to try all the positions at this age and should be shifted from position to position.

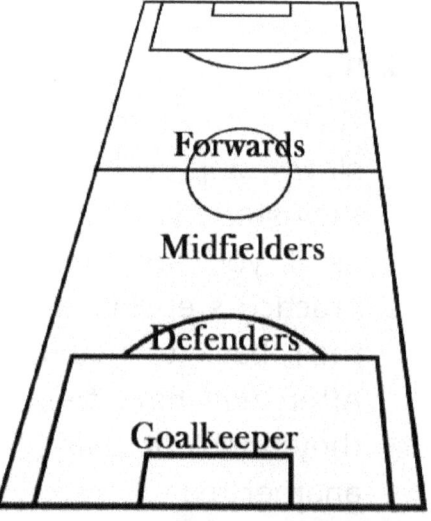

TEACH THE ROLES OF THE GOALKEEPER:

THE JOB OF THE GOALKEEPER:

The Goalkeeper's main job is to stop the ball from getting through the net. Focus is a key strategy, not only when the ball is close, but also when it is on the other end of the field. A keeper can only handle the ball inside his/her own penalty area (the rectangular area in front of and within the goal post).

How a Goalkeeper Catches/Stops a Ball in the air:
1. Keep hands moving together. Both should be behind the ball with thumbs close together.
2. Elbows should be in front of the chest.
3. Get behind the ball. When reaching for a ball, the arms should be extended out (elbows not locked!), the elbows bent as the catch is made, allowing the arms to absorb the speed and energy of the ball. Hands should be in the "W" hand position.
4. The Goalkeeper should be always bouncing on the balls of the feet. On the ground, Goalkeeper should step on foot by the ball and lower one knee close without touching the ground while picking up ball.
5. The ball may need to be hugged to the chest to protect it.

If the ball is on the ground:
The basket catch is used for balls on the ground. The hands are behind the ball, but the pinky fingers are together so the ball is cupped when it rolls in. Fingers

may need to brush the ground to catch the ball. It can be caught with legs straight, knees bent or kneeling.

Drills:

- Practice catching the ball by throwing it back and forth between players.
- Discuss that it is a team effort to protect the ball and not the Goalkeeper's fault if he misses and the other team gets a point.
- Sideways shuffling between cones or quick steps forward and backwards between cones to practice covering the goal area.
- Have one player be the goalkeeper. Divide players up into two sides and set up six cones on either side so each group can race to traverse the cones and try to take a shot into the goal.
- Have the players each take turns protecting the goal while the rest of the team each takes turns dribbling the ball from midfield and trying to shoot a goal. To make it less difficult for the goalkeeper, give him one or two defensemen to help out.

Week 3—Ages 8-10

Goals:

1. Developing a basic understanding of goal kick, corner kick, kick off and throw in and when the ball is in or out of play.
2. Third shielding position
3. Beginning Fakes:
   - The Fake Pullback
   - Cut Back

Teaching Tool:

DEVELOPING A BASIC UNDERSTANDING OF GOAL KICK, CORNER KICK, KICK OFF AND THROW IN AND WHEN THE BALL IS IN OR OUT OF PLAY:

BASIC RULES OF SOCCER:

The Game: At the start of play, there is a kick-off. All the players must be on their defending side of the field. Only the player kicking off is allowed inside the center circle. After the kick-off, the ball will be played until it goes out of bounces or the referee calls a penalty. The ball must

completely cross the boundary to be out of bounds.
- You can't intentionally touch the ball with your hands or arms unless you are a goalie.
- You can't foul another player:
    - Fouling is: Tripping, pushing, unsportsmanlike, behavior, touching the ball with hands or arm.
    - Penalty kicks may be awarded to the team that received the foul
    - Offending player may receive a yellow or red card.

Kick off - At the beginning of a period, at the beginning of a game or after a goal is made. Ball is placed on the center mark and kicked by one team. Until the ball crosses the line, players from the attacking team may not cross the central mark and players from the defending team must be at least 10 yards from the ball. The kicker cannot kick the ball again until another player has touched the ball.

Throw in - When the whole of the ball has passed over a touch line, either by air or on the ground, it is put back into play by a throw in at the point the ball crossed the line by a player of the team opposite of the last one who touched it. The player must face the playing field with part of each foot on the touchline or on the ground outside the touchline. Part of each foot must be on the ground. Both hands must be used to throw the ball and ball must be held behind and over the head.

Corner Kick - When the ball passes completely over the

defending team's goal line and was last touched by a *defending player* and a goal was not scored. It is put back into play by a player of the attacking team from the corner of the field nearest to where the ball crossed.

Goal Kick- When the ball goes out of the defending team's goal line, was last touched by the *attacking team* and there was no score, it is put back into play by the defending team. They may place the ball anywhere within their Goal Box (including on the line) and then kick it.

Penalty kick: When a foul occurs in the penalty area, the fouled team is awarded a penalty kick.

Off Sides - The offensive player is offside if they are nearer to the opponent's goal line than both the second to last and last opponent and the soccer ball.

Teaching Tool:

Go over the simple step across from practice 1 and the roll from practice 2, then teach the 3rd shielding practice:

1. **Simple step across** - The player steps over the ball to put either one or both legs between the ball and an incoming opponent. Player is trying to place themselves in the best position to pass to teammates.
2. **The roll** - Player moves the ball around either with the side of the foot or the sole of the foot.

The third shielding practice is:

3. **The pull-back-** The pullback move is used when an opposing team player is coming in quickly, so the ball is basically pulled or rolled to one side using the sole of the foot. Start with the ball between your feet. Make a fake motion of kicking the ball with the right foot. Then instead of kicking, stop the ball with the bottom of your shoe to the top of the ball. Then pull back the ball by scraping the cleats backwards to get the ball rolling to the right and behind.

Teaching Tool:

TEACH BEGINNING FAKES:

1. Fake Pullback

Player fakes a kicking motion, but stops with cleats on top of the ball. Then the player pulls back the ball by "scraping" cleats backwards to get the ball rolling behind. Player can turn clockwise or counterclockwise to face the ball again.

- **Drill**: Lay out a line of cones. Have players dribble ball through cones. At each cone, have them stop and perform a pullback.

2. The Cut Back.

While dribbling to the left of an opponent, player uses the inside of the foot to cut the ball back behind the body. Player plants the left foot to the side of the ball and then brings the right foot up to cut the ball back.

- **Drill**: Lay out a line of cones. Have players dribble

ball through cones. At each cone, have them stop and perform a cut back.

Drills:

- Place cones on the field at each different position. Walk to the cones and explain each of the different positions. Players will be able to try all the positions at this age and should be shifted from position to position.
- Play Soccer Tag-Have one player dribble the ball and try to tag the others with the ball. Whoever gets tagged, is "it".
- Play a scrimmage game. Every 2-3 minutes, have players change positions with your calling out the names of the positions each will take. Make sure all the players get a short chance at playing goalkeeper.

Week 4—Ages 8-10

Goals:
1. Team support when defending and attacking and giving each other space to play.
2. Fourth Shielding Practice
3. Beginning Fakes
4. Lunge

Teaching Tool:

Go over the Shields—simple step across, the roll and the pullback from previous practices:

1. **Simple step across** - The player steps over the ball to put either one or both legs between the ball and an incoming opponent. Player is trying to place themselves in the best position to pass to teammates.
2. **The roll** - Player moves the ball around either with the side of the foot or the sole of the foot.
3. **The pull-back–** With the pullback move, the ball is pulled or rolled to one side using the bottom of the foot. Start with the ball between your feet. Make a fake motion of kicking the ball with the right foot. Then instead of kicking, stop the ball with the bottom of your shoe to the top of the ball. Then pull back the ball by scraping the cleats backwards to get the ball rolling to the right and behind.

Teach the final Shielding Practice:

4. **The circle turn** - There are two types of circle turns - one by using the inside of the foot and one by using the outside of the foot. The ball is tapped with the foot in the opposite direction of the opponent and in a circle.

Teaching Tool:

TEACH BEGINNING FAKES:

1. Fake Pullback

Player fakes a kicking motion, but stops with cleats on top of the ball. Then the player pulls back the ball by "scraping" cleats backwards to get the ball rolling behind. Player can turn clockwise or counterclockwise to face the ball again.

- **Drill**: Lay out a line of cones. Have players dribble ball through cones. At each cone, have them stop and perform a pullback.

2. The Cut Back.

While dribbling to the left of an opponent, player uses the inside of the foot to cut the ball back behind the body. Player plants the left foot to the side of the ball and then brings the right foot up to cut the ball back.

- **Drill**: Lay out a line of cones. Have players dribble ball through cones. At each cone, have them stop and perform a cut back.

3. Lunge

Player swings the foot just in front of the ball to the outside. Then player fakes going to the left by lunging with the left foot to the left. Ball is then taken away with

the outside of the right foot to the right.
- **Drill**: Lay out a line of cones. Have players dribble ball through cones. At each cone, have them stop and perform a lunge.

COACHING 11-17 YEAR OLDS

COACHING 11-17 YEAR OLDS

The main objectives of coaching players 11 through 17 years of age is giving them a more in-depth understanding of the rules of the game, reinstating proper kicking and dribbling of the ball and developing both basic techniques of keeping the ball in possession, shield, faking and learning to work together as a team.

At this age, they will learn the basic concepts of goalkeeping, protecting the goal and an overall awareness of what is going on around them on the field. They will also be guided in understanding goal kick, corner kick, kick off and throw in and when the ball is "in" or "out" of play. Youth ages 11-17 should be aware of all aspects of the game while playing and maintaining their position and also understand the role of their own position on the field. This will tell them how they connect to the rest of the team.

THE LESSONS:

The lessons are divided into four weeks. Each week, players will be introduced to a new goal. It is *not* imperative that they accomplish the goals to move on, only that they follow the principles and have a basic understanding of them through the games and exercises. There is no need to spend more than 2-3 minutes talking about the goals to the players. They will learn them over time and by playing the games. In other words, we want the players to learn by having fun!

Coach Guidelines — Vinton County Soccer League

Remember that players learn goals at different stages. Some learn a certain goal early and others may take more time. Every player may not be able to accomplish all the goals by the end of the season. Our main purpose is to offer the goal and let them learn by having fun.

- The basic goals you are attempting to achieve with this age group are:
- Reinstating the proper way to shoot and dribble the ball
- Understanding possession of the ball and how to stop an oncoming ball.
- Developing techniques to keep possession of the ball while dribbling including shielding and faking.
- Developing an understanding of goal kick, corner kick, kick off and throw in and when the ball is in or out of play.
- Learning to work together as a team in passing and defending.
- Understand the role of goalkeeper - using hands and body to defend goal.
- Team support when defending and attacking and giving each other space to play.
- Reading game while keeping their position.
- Team work!

Ball Size: 5
Recommended Field Sizes: 110 X 70 or 100 X 60
Goal Size: 8 feet high X 24 wide
Match Duration—4 (8-10 minutes)

Field 7 x 7

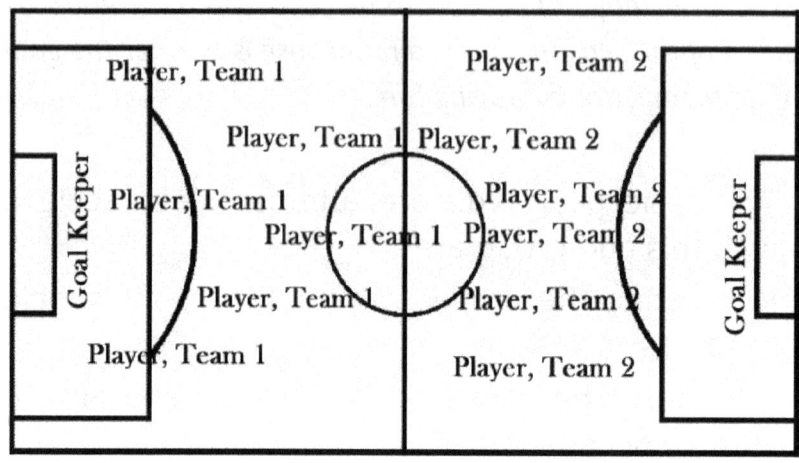

Field 5 X 5

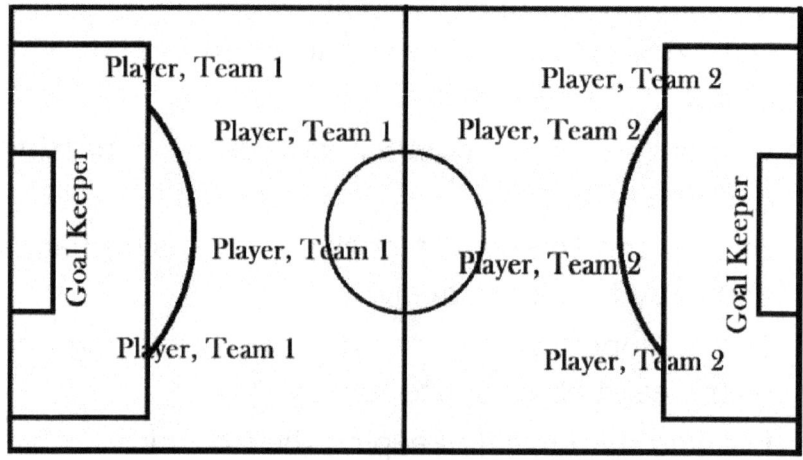

Week 1—Ages 11-17

Goals:
1. Warm up
2. Go over the proper way to dribble, kick and pass the ball.
3. Learn how to stop the ball -Stopping the ball when it is coming to the player using the foot. Then dribbling the ball after it is stopped.
4. Understanding possession of the ball-Don't hold back when you run toward the ball even if an opponent is almost to the ball
5. Learn first Shield steps in Shielding :

Teaching Tool:

HOW TO DRIBBLE A SOCCER BALL:

One of the basic fundamentals of soccer is moving the ball from one place to another.

- Tap the ball back and forth with the insides of your shoe to push the ball forward.
- Knees should be bent
- Arms should be out for balance and to keep defenders out of the player's space
- Eyes should not be on the ball

To move the ball in a different direction:
Touch the ball with the outside of the foot with toe slightly up and ankle locked.

Teaching Tool:

HOW TO KICK A SOCCER BALL:

THE BASIC KICK:
1. Look up quickly before kicking the ball
2. Look back at the ball
3. Take a large stride and plant the foot you are not going to use to kick the ball.

4. Swing your arms
5. Bring your kicking leg back, lock your ankle and kick. Use the top surface area of your shoe (big toe knuckle) just before the area the laces begin.

A few other ways to kick the ball:

- **Instep** – To strike with power, use the top surface of the foot where the shoe laces begin.
- **Inside of the Foot** – Kick with the inside of the foot for more defined accuracy.
    - Or wrap the foot around the ball, cupping it.
- **Outside of the Foot** - Use the outer surface of the front part of your foot to strike the center of the ball.
- **The Volley** – a Strike when the ball is coming to you and out of the air.
- **The Toe** If you have to stretch for the ball, use the toe to kick it.

Drill:
- Line up players across from each other and have them kick the ball back and forth to each other
- Line up cones in front of the goal and have players dribble through the cones and shoot from different distances.

Teaching Tool:

Passing the Ball:

Players work together, kicking the ball short and long distances to an opponent's goal.

1. **Standard Pass**: For shorter distances. Player turns the hip outward and lifts leg to the side. The ball is passed with the inside of the foot. Body is pointed toward the teammate. This is the pass used most often when the ball is on the ground.
2. **Lofted Pass**: For longer distances. Place the left foot. Kick the bottom of the ball with the right at the knuckle of the big toe.
3. **Push Pass**: Player uses the instep of the cleat (at the arch) and along the arch to push the ball in a forward motion.

Teaching Tool:

HOW TO STOP A BALL:

Players can stop a ball with: the inside or outside of the foot, heel, shin, thigh, stomach, chest, shoulder or head.

Upper Body: When the ball impacts with the upper body from the air, relax the part of your body which is going to stop the ball and move slightly backwards to absorb the impact.

The Feet: When the ball is ready to impact with the foot, lean slightly on the opposite leg. AS the ball reaches the cleat, move the foot gently back to absorb the impact. Player can stop the ball with the inside of the foot, the outside of the foot or by absorbing the impact with the toe on top of the ball.

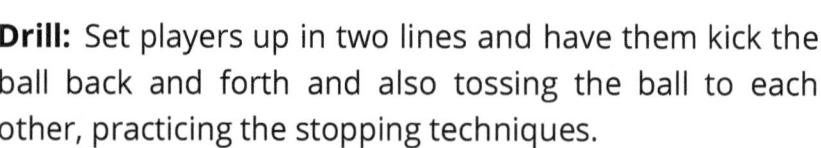

Drill: Set players up in two lines and have them kick the ball back and forth and also tossing the ball to each other, practicing the stopping techniques.

Teaching Tool:
Possession of the Ball

It is important for players to learn to be strong defenders and also, to not fear going after the ball if it is in another's possession. In other words, players should not stop just because an opponent has the ball.

Drill:

Stand halfway across the field with your foot on the ball, barely holding it. Have each player, one by one, come up and kick the ball from your foot. Do not try to stop them. After they have done this a couple times, start at the center of the field, dribble the ball toward them and have each player run toward you and take it away. Next, pair them up and let them practice attacking and taking the ball.

Teaching Tool:

First Steps of Shielding:

BASIC SHIELDING

It is important to learn good shielding techniques to keep the opponent from stealing the ball, and to protect the space around the player.

Shields are used when it is simply too difficult to continue dribbling the ball past an opponent (there are either too many opponents near or the opponent blocks the course).

The basic shielding posture is:
- Knees should be bent
- Arms bent and out to sides

There are four types of shielding. The first two to learn is:

1. **Simple step across** - The player steps over the ball to put either one or both legs between the ball and an incoming opponent. Player is trying to place themselves in the best position to pass to teammates.
2. **The roll** - Player moves the ball around either with the side of the foot or the sole of the foot.

Drills:

Pair up the players and have them stand five steps away. Have one of the pair stand in front of a cone about a foot away while the second comes up to take it away. This should be an easy take. Now have the cone holder stand in front of the cone to protect it but they can't move their feet. Another easy take. Last, have the cone holder stand on the edges of the cone with their arms out in a shielding position and their legs bent slightly. Have their opponent try to take the cone this time. It will be very difficult and an easy lesson in shielding the ball closely.

Game: Use two rows of cones and divide a 30x30 grid vertically into three equal size rectangles. Play 3v3. Each team can have one player in each of the three zones. They can receive, pass and dribble but can't go out of their zone. They must run and get open and mark defensively inside their zone. If they do, they concede a free kick wherever they step over the line. After a few scores, swap the players to a new zone and a new 1v1 match-up.

Week 2—Ages 11-17

Goals:
1. Warm up
2. Understand the roles of each position
3. Understand the role of goalkeeper
4. Learn Second Shield steps in Shielding:
    - The Pullback
    - The Circle Turn

Teaching Tool:

SOCCER POSITIONS EXPLAINED:

Each player position has a specific task, from defending against opponent attacks to scoring.

Forwards are positioned nearest to the opposing team's goal. They are the attackers used to move the ball forward and score goals. Forwards need to be fast dribblers and be agile.

Midfielders play the middle field. Their position is both offensive and defensive. They must be able to dribble the ball and pass to the forwards and also stop an opponent's attack.

Defenders are the closest to their own goal. Their job is to stop the other team from scoring a goal. Strong kicks are a must for defenders to get the ball out of the scoring area.

Goalkeepers protect the goal and the last line of defense against the opposing team scoring.

Teaching Tool:

THE JOB OF THE GOALKEEPER:

The Goalkeeper's main job is to stop the ball from getting through the net. Focus is a key strategy, not only when the ball is close, but also when it is on the other end of the field. A keeper can only handle the ball inside his/her own penalty area (the rectangular area in front of and within the goal post).

How a Goalkeeper Catches/Stops a Ball in the air:

1. Keep hands moving together. Both should be behind the ball with thumbs close together.
2. Elbows should be in front of the chest.
3. Get behind the ball. When reaching for a ball, the arms should be extended out (elbows not locked!), the elbows bent as the catch is made, allowing the arms to absorb the speed and energy of the ball. Hands should be in the "W" hand position.
4. The Goalkeeper should be always bouncing on the balls of the feet. On the ground, Goalkeeper should step on foot by the ball and lower one knee close without touching the ground while picking up ball.
5. The ball may need to be hugged to the chest to protect it.

If the ball is on the ground:

The basket catch is used for balls on the ground. The hands are behind the ball, but the pinky fingers are together so the ball is cupped when it rolls in. Fingers may need to brush the ground to catch the ball. It can be caught with legs straight, knees bent or kneeling.

Drills:
- Practice catching the ball by throwing it back and forth between players.
- Put players in teams of threes. Line them up with a goalkeeper in the center and approximately ten feet between the players. Have the first player kick the ball at the goalkeeper. As soon as he catches or misses, the second player on the opposite shoots at the goalkeeper.
- Discuss that it is a team effort to protect the ball and not the Goalkeeper's fault if he misses and the other team gets a point.
- Sideways shuffling between cones or quick steps forward and backwards between cones to practice covering the goal area.
- Have one player be the goalkeeper. Divide players up into two sides and set up six cones on either side so each group can race to traverse the cones and try to take a shot into the goal.

Teaching Tool:

Go over the simple step across from and the roll, then teach the final two shielding practices:

1. **Simple step across** - The player steps over the ball to put either one or both legs between the ball and an incoming opponent. Player is trying to place themselves in the best position to pass to teammates.
2. **The roll** - Player moves the ball around either with the side of the foot or the sole of the foot.

3. **The pull-back-** The pullback move is used when an opponent is coming in so quickly that it will be hard to step across the ball in time to shield it, so the ball is basically pulled or rolled to one side using the sole of the foot. Start with the ball between your feet. Make a fake motion of kicking the ball with the right foot. Then instead of kicking, stop the ball with the bottom of your shoe to the top of the ball. Then pull back the ball by scraping the cleats backwards to get the ball rolling to the right and behind.
4. **The circle turn** - There are two types of circle turns - one by using the inside of the foot and one by using the outside of the foot. The ball is tapped with the foot in the opposite direction of the opponent and in a circle.

Drill:

Using two lines of cones in a straight line, have the players dribbling around each and practice each shielding technique at different intervals.

Game: Play a regular small-sided soccer game, but instead of each team having a goal set up one goal in the middle of the playing area. Teams can score by shooting the ball through the goal from either direction. First time, don't use a goalkeeper. After a few minutes, let the players take turns keeping goal.

Week 3—Ages 11-17

1. Warm up
2. Developing a basic understanding of goal kick, corner kick, kick off and throw in and when the ball is in or out of play.
3. Go over the 4 steps to shielding.
4. Begin Learning fakes:
   - Turn with Pullback
   - Turn away with Pullback

Teaching Tool:

BASIC RULES OF SOCCER:

The Game: At the start of play, there is a kick-off. All the players must be on their defending side of the field. Only the player kicking off is allowed inside the center circle.

After the kick-off, the ball will be played until it goes out of bounces or the referee calls a penalty. The ball must *completely* cross the boundary to be out of bounds.

- You can't intentionally touch the ball with your hands or arms unless you are a goalie.
- You can't foul another player:
  - Fouling is: Tripping, pushing, unsportsmanlike, behavior, touching the ball with hands or arm.
  - Penalty kicks may be awarded to the team that received the foul
  - Offending player may receive a yellow or red card.

Kick off - At the beginning of a period, at the beginning of a game or after a goal is made. Ball is placed on the center mark and kicked by one team. Until the ball crosses the line, players from the attacking team may not cross the central mark and players from the defending team must be at least 10 yards from the ball. The kicker cannot kick the ball again until another player has touched the ball.

Throw in - When the whole of the ball has passed over a touch line, either by air or on the ground, it is put back into play by a throw in at the point the ball crossed the line by a player of the team opposite of the last one who touched it. The player must face the playing field with part of each foot on the touchline or on the ground outside the touchline. Part of each foot must be on the ground. Both hands must be used to throw the ball and ball must be held behind and over the head.

Corner Kick - When the ball passes completely over the defending team's goal line and was last touched by a *defending player* and a goal was not scored. It is put back into play by a player of the attacking team from the corner of the field nearest to where the ball crossed.

Goal Kick- When the ball goes out of the defending team's goal line, was last touched by the *attacking team* and there was no score, it is put back into play by the defending team. They may place the ball anywhere within their Goal Box (including on the line) and then kick it.

Penalty kick: When a foul occurs in the penalty area, the fouled team is awarded a penalty kick.

Off Sides - The offensive player is offside if they are nearer to the opponent's goal line than both the second to last and last opponent and the soccer ball.

Teaching Tool:

The 4 Steps to Shielding:

Shielding the ball keeps the opponent from stealing the ball. The four basic shielding moves are:

1. **Simple step across** - The player steps over the ball to put either one or both legs between the ball and an opponent. Player is trying to place themselves in the best position to pass to teammates.
2. **The roll** - Player moves the ball around either with the side of the foot or the sole of the foot.
3. **The pull-back-** The pullback move is used when an opponent is coming in so quickly that it will be hard to step across the ball in time to shield it, so the ball is pulled or rolled to one side using the sole of the foot. Start with the ball between your feet. Make a fake motion kicking the ball with the right foot. Instead of kicking, stop the ball with the bottom of the shoe to the top of the ball. Pull ball back by scraping cleats backward to get the ball rolling to the right and behind.
4. **The circle turn** - There are two types of circle turns - One-using the inside of the foot. One-using the outside of the foot. The ball is tapped with the foot in the opposite direction of the opponent and in a circle.

Teaching Tool:

TEACH BEGINNING FAKES:

1. Fake Pullback

Player fakes a kicking motion, but stops with cleats on top of the ball. Then the player pulls back the ball by "scraping" cleats backwards to get the ball rolling behind. Player can turn clockwise or counterclockwise to face the ball again.

- **Drill**: Lay out a line of cones. Have players dribble ball through cones. At each cone, have them stop and perform a pullback.

2. The Cut Back.

While dribbling to the left of an opponent, player uses the inside of the foot to cut the ball back behind the body. Player plants the left foot to the side of the ball and then brings the right foot up to cut the ball back.

- **Drill**: Lay out a line of cones. Have players dribble ball through cones. At each cone, have them stop and perform a cut back.

More Drills:

- Play a scrimmage game. Every 2-3 minutes, have players change positions with your calling out the names of the positions each will take. Make sure all the players get a short chance at playing goalkeeper.

Week 4—Ages 11-17

Goals:

1. Warm up
2. Team support when defending and attacking and giving each other space to play.
3. Begin Learning fakes:
   - Fake Kick Inside
   - Fake Kick Outside
   - Step over 180

Teaching Tool:

GREAT FAKES:

- **Fake Kick Inside (Pretend to kick, instead kick to inside or outside)**
- **Fake Kick Outside**

While ball is being dribbled, the left foot is planted near the ball and the right is wound up as if to kick. Instead of kicking the ball, the right leg is brought down in a chopping motion to cut the ball to either direction. If it is moved with the outside of the foot, it is a fake kick outside. If it is moved with the inside, it is a fake kick inside.

The Step over.

When dribbling the ball toward the opponent, player steps *over* the ball with the right foot and appears to be heading left. (Foot will land to the left of the ball) As the opponent goes to the left, the outside of the right foot should be equal to the ball and is used to push the ball to the right.

Step over 180

Player starts with ball between feet. With weight on the left leg, the right foot is swung over the ball while turning counter clockwise to the left. Then, the right foot is placed down on the left side of the ball. Finally, the right foot is used to pivot, spin around with the left foot back toward the ball. After turning 180 degrees, take the ball with the left foot and move in either direction.

Drill:

- Line up cones and have players dribble through, stopping at the end cone to perform each fake.
- Make 3 teams (Green-Blue-Red) 4v4v4 or 5v5v5 or 6v6v6 in Square grid about 25 x 25. Vary the size for player numbers and ability. One team starts as the defenders and the other two teams play keep away. When the defenders win the ball, the team color which was responsible for losing the ball become the defenders. You can give a goal for X number of consecutive passes.

We want to thank all the coaches for everything they do for the players. It takes a lot of time and patience and dedication to help build a league. Without you, there isn't a team. Without you, there isn't a league. Without you, there is one less kid who gets to be a part of something—a team, a league, something big.

Thank you!

www.ingramcontent.com/pod-product-compliance
Lightning Source LLC
Chambersburg PA
CBHW070549090426
42735CB00013B/3126